GATEKEEPERS

LET'S TALK ABOUT TEACHING

TAMMY MᶜMORROW

FOREWORD BY JIM FREDRICKSEN

ISBN: 1542952026
ISBN-13: 978-1542952026

Cover design by 4thirteen Designs
About the Author photography by Rosie Nary Photography

This book is dedicated to the brave teachers who stand at the doors of their classrooms and guard against any practice or mandate that is not in their students' best interests. They are the gatekeepers, and this book is for them.

CONTENTS

FOREWORD
By Jim Fredricksen

When I was a relatively new teacher, I remember once complaining to a school secretary about my students. "They just don't seem to be engaged or enjoying their time with me. It's such a drag."

The secretary, who happened to be my mom, let me vent for a few minutes about this student or that one, but then she had enough. "You know," she said, "you're the adult in the classroom. If you're not enjoying the classroom, then it's your fault."

The words stung because I knew them to be true. I had cultivated a classroom culture of control, which drained it of curiosity or creativity or joy.

Days later, I asked Martha, the art teacher down the hallway, if I could visit her classroom during a prep period. "Do you mind if I just see how things work in your classroom?" I didn't even finish my question before she said, "Of course. Anytime."

Martha's classroom was colorful and full of life. Students huddled around her desk for a few minutes to see her try a particular technique, and then they would head out to work on their own pieces and techniques. She made risk-taking not only permissible, but desirable. Martha would lead students in conversations about one another's attempts, teaching them how artists give and receive feedback. If an artist finished one piece, then Martha prompted them to move on to the next. If an artist needed more time to revise, then Martha offered the structure and the space for students to see a piece through its end. Students practiced choice and agency and power, all the while creating a community of learners who worked toward applying the principles of perspective, texture, balance, unity, and more.

The culture in Martha's class became my model and my inspiration. For the next few years, I would visit Martha's class off and on, and I would pick her brain about how she organized her curriculum, how she made in-the-moment judgments in her teaching, and how she supported students in order for them to move forward as artists and in their understanding of art. We'd join forces from time-to-time too, such as when we asked my students to choose a piece of their peers' art displayed across our school and to write a piece of fiction or a poem to accompany it or when she would visit my class to listen to writers craft their stories.

I mention Martha and how important she is to me, because reading *Gatekeepers* makes me think Tammy McMorrow could be your Martha. Like Martha, Tammy opens up her classroom, invites you in, and then shares what she notices and how she thinks through all the celebrations and trouble that accompanies her work. Like Martha, Tammy's students are encouraged to take risks and to make learning their own. Like Martha, Tammy creates space for colleagues – like you and me – to make connections, to adapt for our own purposes and contexts, and to join in an ongoing conversation.

I have been thinking a lot about the idea of "hospitality" a lot in recent years. I keep coming back to Henri Nouwen, who wrote in *Reaching Out: The Three Movements of the Spiritual Life*, "Hospitality is not to change people, but to offer them space where change can take place."

Like all the best and most generous colleagues and teachers, Tammy practices hospitality. The book in your hand does not direct you to change – it's not a step-by-step recipe for how to be a teacher; it's not a series of handouts to run off for your students; it's not even something you have to read from front-to-back – she's given you choice there too.

Instead, this book is a space where change is possible.

We all have those moments when we might be pushed in a direction that doesn't ring true or when we've heard a hard truth about our teaching. When these moments pop up, we must turn to mentors and colleagues who inspire us simply by being who they are. Tammy shows us how she does so with the words of authors and educators who inspire her and who help her think about her own challenges.

By writing her blog and this book, Tammy not only models her process for us, but perhaps more importantly, she offers us the gift of time, space, and choice to work our way through our own challenges – "to," as in the words Regie Routman wrote to Tammy, "be you and tell your own story in your own voice."

Tammy invites you in, and then allows you the opportunity to make the place your own.

I can't think of a more generous gift or a more hospitable way of teaching. Enjoy.

INTRODUCTION

We need to be the gatekeepers for sane and sensible practices.

-Regie Routman

"I want to be like you when I grow up," I said. Never before had I been bold enough to speak to her. Nor did I expect a response. It wasn't that I doubted her nature. As a professional who works with teachers and students for a living, I expected her to be warm and friendly. Considering the situation, I simply didn't think a response was necessary. To my surprise, quite promptly she replied, "Be you and tell your story in your own voice. Good luck."

That was the conversation in its entirety, but though rather concise, I giddily thought, "Did *that* just happen?" Twelve words or 100, it didn't matter. Regie Routman had just told me to be me and tell my story. And in my heart her words sounded a bit like, "Yes Tammy, write your book." I'd call that a miracle, considering she had no idea there was a book waiting to be written. Backing up a bit, I admit that calling this discourse a conversation implies that Regie Routman and I actually spoke to one another, which is not altogether how the moment transpired, although wouldn't that be an even better story to tell? Reluctantly, I'm forced to admit that our dialogue took place on her Facebook page, but at least it's forever etched in cyberspace as proof that my educational hero told me to write this book.

Does anyone else experience fleeting random thoughts while taking a shower? I believe that's the setting where the idea of writing a book first flitted through my mind, disappearing as quickly as it arrived. I could have grabbed at it before it vanished, pondering the possibilities. It didn't happen that way. Fear got the best of me. "What could I possibly offer the world of education?" And off the thought went. Maybe that's the way some of our best dreams take shape. They knock on our door when we least expect them, then scurry away before we can see who's there, leaving a faint residue of their existence in our mind's eye. They plant a seed, though, later to return when we're more inclined to accept their company and maybe even long for it. Yet even in the longing, a refrain played in my mind. "Who do you think you are anyway, writing a book? Regie Routman writes books, not Tammy McMorrow," not because I'd heard the words spoken, but because surely this is what the masses must be thinking. Similar to the Israelites entering the promised land full of giants, I was a grasshopper in my own sight. But I've learned that Regie Routman is right. I have a story to tell and a voice worth hearing.

I've been living my story for 23 years in a first-grade classroom in a rural Idaho town. Especially loving the challenges of welcoming six-year olds into the literacy club but lacking the knowledge to meet their varied needs, my journey fortunately took me through doors that transformed my thinking and practices, like Reading Recovery, earning a master's degree in reading, and becoming a National Writing Project Fellow, to name a few. I also became acquainted with the writings of many wise leaders in the field of education and used their books for personal professional development. For 18 of those years, my story was a fairly private one. It wasn't until I started a blog about teaching, called Forever in First, that my pedagogy, opinions, practices, and classroom were let out of the bag, so to speak. Saturday quickly became my favorite day of blogging. I made a habit of using it for a weekly post called Saturday Sayings. I share quotations from my favorite educational gurus, along with my reflections. I voice my opinions and my readers comment with their own. When it comes to blogging and sharing my ideas, these posts filled with quotations and conversations are the ones I am the most proud of. This book is basically a compilation of those Saturday Sayings in a revised form.

You have my permission to make up your own rules as you read. The chapters are in no special order. Close your eyes, open the book to any page, and start there if you'd like, or read it in order from beginning to end. Read it in one day or in one hundred. The only thing I ask is that you grant yourself enough time for reflection. Imagine me saying, "This is my opinion. Now what's yours?" which mirrors the reflective dialogue that occurs on my blog when readers leave their comments. You decide where you'll leave yours. This book is just begging to be written in though, so my hope is that you will add your thoughts to the page, both literally and figuratively. Janice Sullivan, my Reading Recovery trainer and literacy mentor, would often respond to the reading of an educational passage with, "That's what it says. Now what does it really mean?" My hope is that you will respond in a similar fashion while reading the quotations and reflections in this book.

I could not have written this book without the educational gurus who inspire the day-to-day happenings of my classroom. It's based on the foundation of their thoughts, pedagogy, and heart. I'm not ashamed to say that without them this book wouldn't breathe. Natalie Goldberg in *Writing Down the Bones* says, "We are very arrogant to think we alone have a totally original mind. We are carried on the backs of all the writers who came before us." So then, who do I think I am anyway, writing a book? I am really no different than you. I'm a gatekeeper for sane and sensible practices. It's my responsibility to stand guard at the gate of my classroom, putting my life between my students and any practice that might do them harm. To some, that might sound melodramatic. For me, it is my calling. Unsatisfied with my present knowledge and ability to guard the gate, I read, reflect, write, and converse with educational leaders regarding the status quo. I invite you to join the discourse. In reading this book, I hope you feel free to voice your opinions, reflect on your practices, and stand strong with me as we guard the gate.

1. I Am the Teacher

Do you want a guaranteed formula for disappointment in life? Set up the rules of your life so that you have to win every time or have one hundred percent success in order to feel fulfilled.

-Dave Burgess

I am the teacher . . .

who was interviewed on a podcast

who is writing a book

whose classroom vignette was published in a book

whose idea was shared in the *Instructor Magazine*

who posts opinionated thoughts on a blog

who professionally tweets on Twitter

who provides writing PD for other teachers

who has a solid reputation in her district

And yet I am the teacher . . .

who fails on a fairly regular basis

who reads professional books that have yet to find a way into her practice

who struggles with engaging all her learners

who is not up-to-date on the newest children's literature

who struggles to meet everyone's needs

who does not handle every conflict in the classroom with grace

who recognizes that she allows the clock too much influence in her room

who is embarrassed to even speak about some of her struggles

And the list goes on.

The bottom half of my story can be so very suffocating at times that it's difficult to even breathe in the possibility that I can be both teachers at the same time.

I have difficulty acknowledging all that I have accomplished when I am in a state of feeling overwhelmed about the teacher who still battles with foundational concepts like engagement and relationships.

When others sing my praises, the voice inside whispers, "If you only knew."

I'm reminding myself, and maybe someone else as well, to acknowledge and celebrate. Regie Routman says that celebration is at the heart of her best teaching. Maybe it's necessary that teachers celebrate themselves too.

I hope to always be the teacher who does extraordinary things, but I will also always be the teacher who must grow beyond what I know on behalf of the students who continually need my best.

Today, right now, I strive to be okay with the difference between these two teachers, because they can and do coexist.

2. BE A GAS STATION

I try to carry the uniqueness of each child in my head.

-Donald Graves

It was finally Identity Day. The excitement in the air was obvious as students prepared to share about themselves after a week of much thought and preparation. To be honest, it's possible I was even more thrilled than the students. I understood the lasting effects this moment could have on us. Standing alone, but confidently, at the front of the room, each one described his or her passion. Horses, soccer, whales, art. They lifted their accompanying props for all to see and asked for comments or questions when finished. All the while, their teacher was making mental notes about each one's uniqueness and promising herself to commit every passion to memory.

Several months later and I'm still carrying those passions in my head, challenging myself to use them effectively in whatever capacity I can. I will admit the need to up my game in this area. While some students are naturally inclined to love everything about learning, there are a few tough customers who occupy a space in my brain 24/7, because I constantly struggle to find a way to engage their hearts.

One of my goals is to be a better gas station — an analogy I discovered in Kristine Mraz's blog, Kinderconfidential.com. I fill up the gas tank when needed and cheer from the sidelines as off the students go as independent learners. Being a gas station is rewarding for both teacher and student, and it's easier than the exhausting job of dragging children along like a tow truck from skill to skill and standard to standard. I'd venture to say it isn't much fun for the student either. Not to mention, it simply doesn't work.

I still worry about my tough customers, but when I remember the way they shared their passions for horses, animals, and Legos on Identity Day, I make better intentional moves on their behalf. By carrying the uniqueness of each child in my head, by knowing their passions, I can more easily park that tow truck and be the gas station they need me to be.

3. A Lot of Easy

Students need to do lots of reading of easy books for pleasure to become fluent, confident readers.

-Regie Routman

This chapter is dedicated to my first literacy mentor, Janice Sullivan, who passed away last year. Janice trained me in Reading Recovery during my third year of teaching and completely transformed the way I thought about and taught literacy. Her legacy lives on in the reading and writing lives of the children I welcome into the literacy club. We could never thank her enough.

Janice was known for many things, such as rooster calls and snorting, but she also said countless brilliant things like, "A lot of easy reading makes reading easy." Many years later her words still ring true in my practice. She would be proud that I'm intentional about the types of books my readers engage with on a daily basis.

Choosing texts for our readers is a huge task, especially when faced with a room full of students who are as varied as the books we have at our disposal. Numerous research studies strongly recommend getting the right books into the hands of young readers. As Routman states and Allington reiterates, developing readers do not spend nearly enough time simply reading, and the books they are reading independently must be chosen with care. They must be readable and easily understood, not requiring extra supports or scaffolds.

There are times during shared or guided reading when books do require scaffolding. Without proper support, students would not be able to independently read and understand these texts. This provides the teacher a perfect opportunity to intervene and nudge readers to outgrow themselves.

Read-aloud offers a different experience where the text might be complex in a variety of ways but can be enjoyed with the right supports.

Our students need a variety of experiences with a variety of books at a variety of levels, but we must be intentional about the when and the how. In the end, I return to the wise words of Janice Sullivan. If a lot of easy reading makes reading easy, then it's safe to say that a lot of hard reading makes reading hard and thus not enjoyable. If it's not enjoyable, then why try? Too many of our readers are in this boat, and we teachers are the only ones who can change that.

4. UNEXAMINED WALLPAPER

Unexamined wallpaper - classroom practices and institutional policies that are so entrenched in school culture or a teacher's paradigm that their ability to affect student learning is never probed.

-Donalyn Miller

Unexamined wallpaper . . . I'm guessing we all have some hanging around our classrooms, schools, and districts. Whatever the wallpaper represents, we've always done it and never thought twice about whether it's best for kids.

Take for example, spelling tests. Years ago in my classroom, spelling tests fit into the category of unexamined wallpaper. The teachers around me gave them. The parents expected them. The kids just played along. I gave one spelling test to the whole class every week, because that's the way it was done. Then I discovered a different perspective that challenged my thinking, or lack thereof. Are weekly spelling tests best for kids? Should everyone in the class, from the weakest speller to the children who can spell beyond their grade level, be accountable for identical words? Will a Friday spelling test teach them to spell correctly in their daily writing? I experienced a paradigm shift, and as a result, my pedagogy changed. I tore down the old wallpaper and replaced it with something that better met the needs of my students.

That's just one example, but over the years a variety of wallpaper has been yanked down and scraped off the pedagogical walls of my room. Unfortunately, I'm sure unexamined bits and pieces stubbornly remain in places where I've yet to look. In all reality, I'm sure there will never come a day when I'll feel confident that my walls are completely bare. Maybe that's because I yearn to be the teacher who constantly reflects and refines my practices, always asking, "Is this best for my kids?"

5. LESSONS GONE BAD

When the task is too hard, when the children don't thoroughly understand the task, or when the purpose of the task is unclear, the result is often off-task behavior and teacher interruptions.

-Debbie Diller

How many times have I finished a lesson and said to myself, "Well, *that* didn't go so well"? It happens to the best of us, whether we've been teaching for twenty-three years or one. In my opinion, a number of variables can play a part in the demise of a lesson, but I believe Diller makes a good point. If I spend my time fighting off-task behavior and dealing with repeated interruptions, I have a responsibility to reflectively ask myself these three questions:

- Was the task too hard?

- Did I explain and model the task well enough so that the students understood what to do?

- Did I make the purpose of the task clear?

I can witness to the fact that typically my least effective and most frustrating lessons are not the children's fault. Though not easy to admit, their behavior was a direct result of my teaching. Maybe the task was too hard, which can lead to all kinds of off-task issues. Maybe, and I think this is common, they simply didn't know how to do what I wanted them to do. Regie Routman so wisely says, "I do it. We do it. We do it. We do it. You do it." Sometimes I am guilty of sending them off without enough practice to handle the task independently, and thus they do not handle it well at all. Maybe they didn't even know why they were doing what I asked of them. If there is no real-life meaning to the task, it's much easier to get off track. Granted, there are moments when I feel like I do everything right and still don't see the results I want, but most of the time, Diller's words ring true. Resisting the urge to shamefully shake my head and crawl into a hole, I need to reflectively recognize the part I play in those lessons gone bad. Future lessons just might turn out dramatically different if I do.

6. CUT SOME STRINGS

Reading has become schoolwork, not an activity in which students willingly engage outside of school. Teachers tie so many strings to reading that students never develop a pleasurable relationship to reading inside or, regrettably, beyond the classroom.

-Donalyn Miller

Book reports and dioramas. In my day, those were all the rage. I didn't know it at the time, but my teachers were keeping tabs on me. I don't recall learning to love reading by doing either, though. I understand a teacher's need to hold readers accountable, but attaching inauthentic strings to what should be a pleasurable activity turns reading into schoolwork. No wonder some students choose to avoid books when given the chance.

When I think of things required of students, I like to think of them in terms of what I, as an adult, would or would not like. Last summer I read 39 books and not once did I complete a diorama, take a computer test, complete a packet of some sort, write a book report, or fill in a worksheet. I did, on the other hand, talk about what I was reading with friends, make comments on Facebook, rate my books on Goodreads, track down similar books to the ones I most enjoyed, and make a few recommendations as well. I even chose to jot down some of my favorite quotes and make notes about how some of my professional reads could influence my teaching.

How can these adult reading behaviors translate into the classroom? When possible, can teachers use real-world methods of interacting with books to keep tabs on their readers? What would happen to our readers if we teachers created an atmosphere similar to what we as adults enjoy? When possible, let's cut a few strings, let them read, and find out.

7. EXPECT MORE

If you're reading everything your students write, they're not writing enough. Expect more.

-Regie Routman

I tell my students that mistakes are our teachers, and the plural pronoun is aptly chosen, for my own teaching mistakes have been some of my best learning moments. Take for example, the way I taught writing once upon a time.

Every writer every day was allotted one piece of writing paper. When they were finished with their story, they were done. Per my instructions, they then waited for me to visit with them.

How many inept methods can we identify in this scenario? One piece of paper is nowhere near enough space to write a story with a clear beginning, middle, and end. In addition, my writers spent more time waiting than writing, and waiting children will naturally find inappropriate ways to entertain themselves. Thus, I spent too much time putting out fires instead of conferring. In my limited amount of time and my obvious control-freak need to meet with every writer every day, my conferring was a watered-down version, to put it lightly. Oh how I limited my writers.

Thankfully I've learned from my mistakes and set myself free from that micro-management style of teaching writing. Even better, my kids are free too. They write and write and write. I intentionally sit down on my own time and peruse their writing folders, but I feel no pressure to read everything they write. When a writer finishes a piece, there's no need to check in with Miss McMorrow. He can recite one of our favorite writing mantras. "When you're done, you've just begun," and off he goes to start a new piece.

Without a doubt my writers write considerably more than my students did ten years ago. I wouldn't be surprised if the students I teach in ten years from now write even more and better than mine do today. I must continue to expect more.

8. Answers Solve Nothing

Answers, of course, solve nothing.
> -Richard Bach (as cited in Buschman, 2003)

Of all the subjects I teach, math is the one that has evolved the most over the past five years. I have always believed in a conceptual approach, but for most of my career I focused on a checklist of acquired skills and correct answers. If the answer was right, check off that skill and move on. Transitioning towards a problem-solving approach has been pivotal. Yet potential issues remain, as addressed in Buschman's thoughts below.

Children's problem-solving accomplishments can sometimes be characterized as 'unconscious competence.' They can solve problems and communicate their solutions using drawings and manipulatives, but they seem unaware of the thought processes taking place.
> -Larry Buschman

These quotations from Bach and Bushman have challenged my way of thinking and operating as a math teacher. No longer is the correct solution the primary focus. Drawings and the proper use of manipulatives are not even the most sought after goal in a child's mathematics instruction. A mathematician's ability to communicate about his or her problem-solving strategies is proof that worthwhile learning is taking place.

I've made some important changes to my practice that I believe are pushing my mathematicians to communicate better and thus understand better as well. "How do you know?" These four words have transformed the way I think about student work, both correct and incorrect. Their responses reveal mathematical understandings as well as misconceptions. They also provide a space for students to teach each other as they hear multiple explanations and strategies. We no longer just *do* math. We communicate about it. Simply finding the answer and showing the work is not enough. The math talk that kids engage in is where it's at.

9. It's Not Always Easy

As teachers, we must stay cognizant of the future world we are contributing to.

                              -Kristine Mraz and Christine Hertz

My students regularly hear me say, "It's not always easy, but it's important." I spontaneously created this saying one day in my classroom. I decided it was smart enough to repeat, so my students hear it often. Upon reflection, I am realizing that maybe in the past I've given my students the wrong impression about the people I have asked them to be.

Have I inadvertently caused them to believe that working with others is easy?

Doing the right thing when no one is watching is a piece of cake?

Listening to their heart will always feel natural?

These are huge misconceptions, considering we adults struggle with these same issues.

Yet I'm not letting them off the hook. I have a responsibility to this future world I'm sending them into. I am relentlessly teaching my students about integrity, cooperation, character, mindset, and numerous other qualities our world is hungry for. I'm raising the bar high, helping them exercise and develop the right muscles for doing the right thing even when it's not convenient. Though a few already make it look relatively easy, I know life will challenge them with all sorts of opportunities and reasons to do the wrong thing. It will take years of practice to get this right, so we had better start now.

But I must let them know this critical thing and repeat it often:

It's not always easy, but it's important.

10. At My Fingertips

Truth be told, teachers should be responsible for their own PD now.
                    -Will Richardson (as cited in Couros, 2015)

I believe teacher excellence should be at the top of any school district's list of goals. When we put teacher excellence first, our students can't help but benefit. Yet a school district can only do so much for their teachers in this regard. This is why I've put myself in charge of my own professional development. It's not my principal's job, school's job, district's or state's job. No one knows my specific needs like I do. Regardless of any plans these systems have in place to increase teacher excellence, it will forever be my responsibility to do the hard lifting when it comes to making the shift from my point A to my point B.

Eight years ago I started a quote journal. When I read a professional book, which is a cost-effective and feasible method of developing my practice, I highlight and annotate my way through the text. When finished, I don't put that book away until I've written my favorite quotes in my journal.

The authors who write these books make me smarter than I could ever be on my own, and my quote journal provides instant access to their wealth of knowledge. How sad to shelve that kind of wisdom and wonder someday, "Now what exactly did Regie say? Where did I read that?" This journal increases the likelihood that their years of experience will find a way into my teaching. By writing down their pedagogy, it even improves my ability to remember it more clearly, and memorizing has never been a strength of mine. But I've been able to pull up their expertise from memory in discussions when I needed them most.

The thousands of words in my journal have directly influenced my teaching philosophy on everything from spelling to classroom management. When I expect my students to read independently if they complete a task early instead of doing some preordained filler activity, I thank Donalyn Miller for reaffirming the fact that readers read in the edge times. When students don't produce what I intended, I think of Regie Routman's wisdom concerning the gradual release of responsibility. I'm truly inspired by these many words, and what an honor to have it all at my fingertips. It is my own version of professional development.

11. BREAKING THE CODE

Teaching into what they do as writers is a clear pathway for helping them break the code as readers.

-Richard Gentry

How do we improve our reading scores? I typically rely on my Reading Recovery training from twenty years ago to help navigate this question when it is periodically discussed at the school or district level. I was taught that we don't take reading for a ride without taking writing along as well. Without both, breaking the code can be haphazard. They each deserve the place of highest regard in the classrooms and lives of our literacy club members.

So I find myself asking, *What kind of writing instruction do our youngest literacy members receive? Is it possible that the answer to fixing some of our reading issues can be found within the context of writing?*

I believe these are valid questions and ones that Gentry, among others, has spent a considerable amount of energy and thought exploring. I would be remiss not to share some of Gentry's best thoughts on this topic from *Breaking the Code*:

- "Kindergarten writing is a means for ensuring reading success."

- "Working with beginning writers is like fixing the drainpipe under the sink and all of a sudden the dishwasher works because, like the sink and the dishwasher, reading and writing are hooked up to the same system."

- "We must look at both reading and writing. When we leave writing out, we only tell half the story. If we don't look at both, we are destined to make mistakes."

- "Writing in kindergarten is the secret to the reading-writing connection and the solution to successful beginning reading instruction in today's schools."

- "Early writing not only complements the reading program, it ensures early reading success."

- "Early intervention is not an option, it is a necessity."

I've long been on a mission to improve writing instruction in the classroom, but my purpose reaches well beyond the obvious objectives of improving the craft of writing and the thinking it involves. I also believe in writing's tangible effect on reading. If our youngest learners are struggling to understand the reading process, let's put some resources and time into how they're learning to write. It might be just what they need in order to break the code.

12. TWO KINDS

What separates those teachers who "look back on the day" from those who are researchers lies in the notion of change. A researcher considers seriously what he might do differently.

-Regie Routman

My personal life is one of consistency. Every step I make from the time I wake to the time I leave my house for school looks almost identical from one day to the next. I tolerate change, but I do not necessarily appreciate it. That is not the case when it comes to my teaching life. Maybe this is an oversimplification, but I have come to the conclusion that when it comes to change, there are basically two kinds of teachers.

There's the teacher who is typically on the receiving end of change, rarely initiating it on her own. This teacher, whether happily or not, seldomly has a choice. She is pushed along by the waves of change simply because change happens and happens often in the educational system. Sometimes this kind of change proves to be helpful and sometimes not, but most likely this teacher is stuck with it regardless.

Then there's the teacher who is seeking out change and creating it for herself. This teacher isn't waiting for unavoidable mandates from oftentimes faceless people who will never set foot in her classroom. Instead, she is constantly searching out instructional improvements as a result of her own daily research. She's seeking, reading, and reflecting. With that kind of perspective comes meaningful and purposeful change. I want to be the second teacher — to be a creator of change instead of simply letting it push me around.

13. THE PRACTICE OF MATHEMATICS

Traditionally mathematics has been taught in our schools as if it were a dead language. It was something that past, mostly dead, mathematicians had created — something that needed to be learned, practiced, and applied. When the definition of mathematics shifts toward "the activity of mathematizing one's lived world," the constructive nature of the discipline and its connection to problem solving becomes clear.

-Catherine Fosnot and Maarten Dolk

I have nothing against my past math teachers, but it's safe to say that in my world, math was something created by dead mathematicians. I memorized their thoughts and applied them to page 134. I got A's in math, but that doesn't mean I fully understood what I was doing. I wasn't necessarily *doing* the practice of mathematics.

Fortunately I'm part of a movement in my state to bring math instruction to life. I heard one math workshop instructor liken math to Language Arts. Language Arts is not just punctuation, grammar, or word choice. Language Arts is putting those things into practice by putting pen to paper and writing for real purposes. Math is not just skills, facts, algorithms, and procedures. Math is putting those things into the practice of mathematics by problem solving, modeling, and communicating.

For too long, math has been about skills, facts, algorithms, and procedures. I don't believe we've shown our students that they're actually supposed to use those things as tools to mathematize their own world. They're supposed to practice mathematics, just like they would practice writing, to see that they're creating math and making sense of it, not leaving the job to some dead mathematicians from long ago.

I haven't fully figured out how to make this happen, but the quote above challenges me to pursue ways to help my mathematicians *do* the practice of mathematics. When I present a problem with personal context to my students and say, "Solve it in a way that makes sense to you," I think I'm on the right track. They grapple with real-world problems, solve them in their own ways, and then teach their solutions to others. Math is alive and well in those moments, created by the hands of first-grade mathematicians. I have a feeling those dead mathematicians of long ago would be proud.

14. START THERE

What matters most to this child? Start there.

-Regie Routman

I see how he plays with the bottom of his shoe when I'm reading a picture book. Or if it's not his shoe, it's something else, while we're doing shared reading. I see how he barely moves his lips or completely ignores us when we count to 100 during a fun math brain break. I see how he tries to get a spot at the back of the group where he thinks I don't see him. I see how little effort he gives and how little interest he shows with most everything we do. I see how after two years of kindergarten he still needs every concept I'm teaching. I see how he's surrounded by so many who seem eager to learn, whether the content is easy or hard.

What I don't see is an eager fire in his eyes, a purpose to his motions, a need for more knowledge. I don't feel him willingly following me on this journey. Instead it seems like I'm dragging him along. He is indeed a mystery, and yet this is nothing new. Every year I ask myself how to engage the one who refuses to meet me halfway. I know Routman's advice is part of the answer to this ever-present dilemma. "What matters most to this child? Start there."

I see him on the edges, wishing I would dig a bit deeper. Wishing I'd find his passions. Wishing I'd create an opportunity for him to access this thing we call school.

Wishing I'd see that, indeed, he is full of greatness.

15. LESS PARENT-DEPENDENT

Schools must work for all children – regardless of which parents the children got. So this is the first challenge of American education. Designing schools that are less parent-dependent.

-Richard Allington

In my first encounter with parents at the beginning of the year, I give them an apple with this note: *An apple for the teacher is really nothing new, except when you remember that parents are teachers too. You and I will make a great team. Thanks for letting me be part of your child's journey. Miss McMorrow*

When I invite parents to join my team, I don't expect them to deal with packets of homework or time-consuming worksheets. I simply ask them to make a daily investment in reading at home — to listen to their children read, celebrate often, use the library as a vital resource, be a reading mentor — and I offer them all the support and resources I can.

Even though I wholeheartedly believe in beseeching parents to be that all-important first teacher to their child, and I'd be remiss if I didn't invite them to be on my team, every year there are handfuls of readers who do all or most of their reading exclusively at school. Yet, as Allington states, I must work for all children in my room regardless of their parents.

Allington rarely beats around the bush, especially when it comes to teacher excellence. If I understand him correctly, he's saying that the instruction in my classroom must be so effective that what happens or doesn't happen at home won't make or break us. The success of my readers, all readers, is highly dependent on what takes place in my classroom. I have a responsibility to be a joyful reading mentor, to share irresistible books with my students, to give them access to enormous amounts of books, to provide them with ample time to practice their skills in context, to make choices, and to talk with others readers. These things, and more, can make a difference for all readers, especially those who don't have the same quality literacy experiences at home.

Some might say that Allington's request is a lofty one and I get that, but I do think he's right. I wholeheartedly believe parents should be involved and it pays off when they are, but what will I do when they aren't?

16. Cool to Ask Questions

Smart teachers make it "cool" for students to ask questions.
                                                    -Regie Routman

This year I'm part of a cohort of teachers called The Idaho Coaching Network. We met for the first time in early August for three days of professional development. As I sat and soaked up all I could from our four coaches, I took mental notes about the quality teaching strategies they were demonstrating. I found myself intrigued by the way one of the coaches repeatedly used this phrase:

What questions do you have about . . . ?

Without fail, she would ask that question after she finished teaching or giving directions. The frequent use of these words let me know it was cool to ask my own questions, to ask for clarification, or to admit a misunderstanding.

I also made note of her wording. Whereas in my classroom the phrase would sound more like, "Do you have any questions?" there is an element of intentionality in her wording that, though subtle, seems important and powerful. The assumption is that asking questions is not only welcome, but expected.

After hearing her ask this question repeatedly throughout our three days together, I made a goal to do the same with my students. I've done a decent job and plan on making it a habit, as it is with my coach. When given the chance, even first graders have insightful questions to ask and often help clear up misunderstandings or fill in gaps that I missed. *Can we choose our own partners? What do we do when we finish?* Learning that it's cool to ask questions is the message I want them to hear loud and clear.

17. No Secrets

Students can go a lifetime and never see another person write, much less show them how to write.

-Donald Graves

My memory rarely serves me well. Ask me a question about my past, and I might defer to my cousin Laurie for the answer. Though memories often fail me, I don't recall ever watching a teacher authentically write or compose in front of me. Wouldn't this be akin to showing someone like myself, who lacks sewing skills, a beautifully crafted quilt and then saying, "Now you go make one just like it." I require more than show and tell. I need to see the process first. I believe this is similar to what we're asking of our writers when all we show them is finished pieces. A lifetime is a long time for our young writers to live without seeing their teachers model writing in front of them.

So why should our writers see us write in front of them?

- They need to see it's normal and okay to struggle with any and every part of the process.
- They need to see writers use strategies to overcome their struggles.
- They need to see how writers cross out, mess up, and revise on the go.
- They need to see how writers make choices.
- They need to see the joy writers experience when ideas and words click.

Why don't we write in front of our writers?

- We're fearful.
- We're embarrassed.
- We lack confidence.
- We're unaware of its importance.

Writing in front of anyone, even a first grader, can indeed be intimidating. I rarely get the words right on the first try and openly sharing that struggle is difficult. But that's exactly what our writers need to see. Sharing my writing space with my students lets them in on some secrets of writing that shouldn't be secret at all. They'll hopefully go more confidently into their own writing space because I share.

18. Failure or Feedback?

The key to failing without quitting is to shift your paradigm to believe there is no such thing as true failure - only feedback.

-Dave Burgess

I recently discovered a podcast series on Bam!Radio by Jon Harper called "My Bad." Jon interviews educators about their most memorable mistakes — memorable for all the wrong reasons. One principal shared the story of a mishandled teacher evaluation that created irreparable issues. He freely admitted that before he was a good lead learner, he was a bad one. While we teachers are most known for celebrating and sharing our best moments, understandably, we tend to remain fairly quiet about the bad ones. I commend Jon and the many educators he interviews for creating a space where errors can be inspiring, as well.

I don't believe it's human nature to view mistakes as inspiring, at least not my own. Regardless, failure comes my way on a consistent basis. Most of the time I strive to use my mistakes as feedback and fuel to do and be better. I've seen teachers who fight with the bad moments, and the battle prevents them from the kind of reflection that comes from perspective. They can't see the possibilities for change and growth. Nor can they acknowledge their strengths. They're too engrossed in self-criticism as a result of what they view as failure. This is paralyzing.

Instead of stopping me in my tracks, feedback has the potential to propel my practice forward. My students and I are continually benefiting from my failed moments of years gone by. Those experiences have left a positive stamp on my practice. Though I can also think of a few that make me cringe, and for a second am tempted to stop and hover in the moment, I try to embrace the knowledge that I've grown from the feedback.

I'm expecting many more "My Bad" moments. Knowing they don't equal failure but instead create movement forward makes them much more bearable.

19. Just Because it Works

No content standard in any class at any level is more important than nurturing and building a love of learning.

-Dave Burgess

"I have no original thoughts of my own." I periodically borrow these words from my cousin David. I suppose they're not altogether true, but I do often rely on the wisdom of mentors who seem considerably smarter than I could ever be. Having said that, I do take ownership of the following phrase:

Just because it works doesn't mean it's good for kids.

First let's define "works." I imagine many stakeholders would equate "works" with acceptable test scores, since that seems to be the method for proving we teachers are doing our jobs well. If the numbers are acceptable, then the instruction must have been acceptable and our students must be on their way to becoming "lifelong learners," as the vision statement often proclaims. Herein lies the misconception. If children score well but the methods used do not inspire them, they are essentially no better off than before instruction began.

I believe it is possible to drag a class of students to good scores while leaving them blind to the joys of learning. I could most likely spend the majority of my day killing and drilling my students to good fluency reading scores with pure phonics, isolated sight words, decodable reading passages, meaningless worksheets or activities, and then top it off with pointless homework. Yet they would be stripped of the joy that comes from listening to and interacting with irresistible read-alouds, reading independently, or engaging in book club discussions with real live books in their hands. These students might receive good fluency scores, but they won't be in love with books. Most likely the opposite will be true.

As Burgess says, building a love of learning in our students takes priority over anything else, and our instruction must reflect that. What indeed are we nurturing?

Test scores or students?

20. Rigor - Use Caution

Let's be careful with this word "rigor."

-Dave Burgess

I firmly believe in high expectations. Heroes of my profession, like Donald Graves and Regie Routman, have made it clear that expectations must be high and are rarely high enough. Having said that, I'd be willing to bet that both Graves and Routman would echo Burgess' cautionary thought about the word "rigor."

The word put a bad taste in my mouth the first moment I heard it used to describe what should take place in my classroom. After reading its definition in Burgess' book, *Teach Like a Pirate*, it's no wonder I had that reaction. These synonyms offered by Burgess tell a grim tale: strictness, severity, stringency, toughness, harshness, rigidity, inflexibility, intransigence. Like Burgess points out in his book, the educational world obviously wouldn't intend for rigor to translate into the classroom exactly as it is defined in the dictionary. Yet I ask, "What exactly does rigor look like?" The possibilities for misinterpretation scare me, as do the potential byproducts.

- Does rigor simply mean ten times more of the same, resulting in quantity over quality?

- Does rigor turn into regurgitation?

- Does rigor lead to meaningless busy work or "stuff" about learning instead of real learning?

- Does rigor produce a stiff and sterile environment?

- Does rigor result in jumping through hoops instead doing what's best for kids?

- Does rigor lead to more high-stakes testing?

Rigor doesn't have to result in any of the above side effects. What if rigor invites kids to rise to the challenge due to content that is irresistible, relevant, and meaningful to their lives and futures? That's surely a conclusion that Graves and Routman would herald. My worry is that the opposite might occur. Rigor's misinterpretation could cause irreparable damage to our system, but more importantly, to our clientele. Use caution. The ever-present question of "Why?" must keep us grounded.

21. A Little Messy

It is important to notice that in any unit of study...the first goal is to invite children to work zealously and with independence, approximating the new kind of writing they are asked to do. One could say, in fact, that the first goal is for children to write bad persuasive letters - and to do so with confidence, zeal, purpose, pleasure, and above all, independence.

-Sarah Taylor

A few years ago I developed and taught a unit on writing realistic fiction. In preparation, I viewed online resources written by elementary teachers. I was taken aback by the excessive use of graphic organizers during the first few days of these units. I found myself wondering, "When do kids actually get to write?" If graphic organizers steal precious time from real writing or don't mirror what adult writers might do in a similar situation, then I question their place within the writing workshop setting. Needless to say, I took a different route when introducing realistic fiction to my writers. On day one my students were giving their best messy approximations.

We writing teachers have permission to put pens into our writers' hands before they even know what they're doing, with the expectation that it won't be pretty. If the assumption is that their first attempts will be bad, then we have no reason to fear what might happen when we invite them to experience an unfamiliar genre. I believe we do a disservice to writers if we wait until we've taught all the finer points of a genre before letting them try or if we give them artificial writing experiences with too many handouts or worksheets before they're allowed to write in context. Writers learn to write by writing, so the goal should be to get them writing from day one of any unit. We needn't fear for the kids' sakes. They rarely know it's messy. We teachers are the ones who fear the start of a unit and the bad pieces that will fill their writing folders for those first few days. We must let go and let them write.

When I begin any writing unit, I have no doubt that when I send the children off to write after my first mini-lesson, the majority of them will write rather bad pieces, but they will do it with confidence, zeal, purpose, pleasure, and independence. That sounds like a perfect place to start.

22. Beat Me to the Punch

Building a community of learners, where students exchange mathematical ideas not only with the teacher but also with one another, should be a goal in every classroom.
                    -National Council of Teachers of Mathematics

Intentionally building a community of learners through discovery and the sharing of ideas is a goal worth striving for. Is it possible that we sometimes forget that students can indeed learn deeply without being explicitly told what to think? Maybe we also forget that they can learn from each other.

I recall a measurement lesson in which I asked students to investigate a numberless clock with only a minute hand. As I moved the minute hand to a spot on the clock, the class determined the number of minutes it was past the hour. Of course, I didn't tell them there was an efficient way of counting the minutes. I knew someone would figure it out. Not surprisingly, Walter chimed in and explained the way he thought we should count them: by 5s of course. We dubbed it, "Walter's Strategy," and I consistently referred to it as such throughout the remainder of the lesson. As we were transitioning to another part of the room for additional practice, Michael urgently told me, "Miss McMorrow, Walter's strategy really *does* work!"

I don't believe I've ever heard them say, "Miss McMorrow's strategy really *does* work!" It's not as though they don't believe me or don't use what I offer, but there's something especially poignant about moments when they learn from each other. It doesn't matter if it's Walter's Strategy or Tatum's Way. They snatch those up with much more urgency than something I mandate. If it comes from a peer, and I celebrate it accordingly, they know it's worth listening to.

They've heard me say many times, "I'm not the only math teacher here today. This room is full of them." Sometimes we simply need to remember to let the students beat us to the punch. The others will listen when we do. Something clicked for Michael when he heard and practiced Walter's strategy, and I'm confident he wasn't the only one.

23. Avoid the Pitfall

Avoid the pitfall of wasting time on busywork — purposeless coloring, centers without meaningful activities, worksheets, and activities we never evaluate. What we ask students to do must be worth their time and ours and contribute to their growing literacy.

-Regie Routman

"How much crying do you allow before you just stop making your 8 year old do homework? I feel like the only thing it is accomplishing is making him HATE creative writing." These are the words of a disheartened mom and cousin of mine. My heart sank at her words. I thought, "We've done it again," and apologized on behalf of my people. I might have also commented "Homework, schmomework." Sometimes we teachers miss the mark, and as a result, kids suffer. She went on to say:

"I think it's a combination of the bulk of homework he is assigned. He's given a packet of math homework for the week and he's supposed to do an online math assignment daily. The online math doesn't take any time, and he doesn't mind it — but the paperwork is usually a large math sheet, which I could consider 'busywork' and a creative writing assignment which is supposed to be a paragraph. It's not that he isn't creative. It really is that he gets SO mad about having to do it. He spends most of his time angry, frustrated, crying, anything but just writing. The thing is . . . I think he would be awesome at writing, if he could write more freely. He is endlessly creative and really intelligent. I feel like these writing cues bore him."

First off, I cringe at the word "packet." Packets most often equal busywork. I'm unsure of what packets and homework accomplish in the lives of little ones, except for, in too many cases, anger, frustration, and tears, like in my cousin's situation. I only ask my children to read every night, and I don't dare call it homework. It's what readers like us love to do.

Secondly, this young boy is immensely talented, creative, and intelligent. He has a wonderful way with words. But from what I can tell, forcing him to write to prompts has turned writing into something it was not meant to be — busywork. Like many young writers, his creativity is stifled when pushed into writing about something he has no personal connection to. The whole experience is obviously stealing his love for writing and learning, instead of igniting a passion for how these things benefit his life.

As Routman reminds us, what we ask of our students must be worth their time and contribute to their growing literacy. Neither is noticeably true in this particular situation. We simply must tread carefully. The pitfalls of busywork will bring out the worst in our students, not the best.

24. Job Number 1

Developing the instructional expertise of every teacher, reorganizing schools so that supporting teacher development is, as they say, Job Number 1, is the only strategy that I can endorse with any enthusiasm and the only one I can find substantial research support for.

-Richard Allington

I've been a blessed teacher to work for outstanding principals who support teacher development. Yet even the best administrator is unable to spend enough quality time in classrooms. We teachers spend the majority of our careers by ourselves without consistent feedback regarding our practice. This is why I have strong opinions about student teachers and the responsibilities we have for their professional development.

Some years ago a talented intern spent a semester in my room. She did a beautiful job with the students. Her classroom management was spot-on. Her instruction was top-notch. In fact, whenever given a suggestion, without fail, she'd incorporate the tip into her next lesson. Yet I remained in the room while she was teaching. It's not that I didn't trust her; She'd proven herself capable. I chose to stay because I knew she'd never have an opportunity like that again. Once she became a teacher, she would spend the remainder of her career on her own. So I positioned myself to ensure she had the privileges and benefits of a mentor, 24/7. Not only did I stay in the room, I chose to avoid my desk, work, and my computer. Instead I watched her lessons and took notes. I was her guide on the side. Her presence in my room was not my invitation to take a vacation from the classroom but a call to step up my game for her benefit. Her professional development was my Job Number 1.

On a side note, I chose to stay for the children, too. No matter how much I trusted her, the children were still under my care and were my responsibility. My presence said, "Yes, Miss Gellings is your teacher and she's in charge, but I'm also invested in what you're doing." My presence also reassured parents that I was overseeing all that was going on in their children's education.

There will come a day for student teachers when they won't have someone like you or me to consistently confirm what they're doing well or offer consistent suggestions for improvement. Our feedback is a once-in-a-lifetime opportunity for these future teachers. That experience has the potential to be some of the best professional development of their career. Let's stick around and give it to them.

25. AN EMPTY ROOM

If your students didn't have to be there, would you be teaching to an empty room?

-Dave Burgess

There are benefits to teaching little people. These are the students who repeatedly pester their parents during the late, hot summer days, wondering if tomorrow is the first day of school. For the most part, first graders want to come, although I have certainly met some who had a different view. I'm not sure what would happen if they didn't have to be there. Would I be teaching to an empty room? It would make for an interesting, yet scary experiment.

Burgess' question spurred my own. What exactly are the qualities of a classroom that would trump all the other facets of life that beg for our students' attention? It seems only natural to answer from the standpoint of my own experience as a student. What would keep me coming back even if I were not required to?

- I feel loved.
- I'm important.
- I'm noticed.
- I feel successful.
- I'm interested in and have a personal, relevant connection to the content.
- I have choice.
- I have a chance to shine in a way that fits my personality and my strengths.
- There's time to apply and practice what I'm learning.
- My attempts and approximations are accepted.
- I'm celebrated.

- I get to do, move, and take breaks.
- My instructor believes in me.

The student in me is likely similar to the ones in my class. I imagine we have similar needs and wants. Are theirs being met? This list, although nowhere near exhaustive, demands reflection. Does my classroom offer my students the chance to experience something they could not live without? Would they show up if they didn't have to? Or would they be overwhelmingly drawn to their Legos, Barbies, and video games?

26. Slow Down to Speed Up

We must be deliberate in September.

-Debbie Miller

I much prefer the antsiness of springtime mixed in with some summer fever to the first several weeks of school when the stark reality of first graders, who are actually kindergarteners in disguise, hits me square between the eyes. Even though there is an anticipation that comes from starting over with a new group of children, the beginning of the school year is always the most challenging for me. The blood curdling scream let out in my room one August afternoon was proof of that, and I promise it wasn't me.

Even though it is the most trying time of the year, it's also without a doubt the most crucial, and one I take very seriously. The remainder of my days with students hinges on what I do and don't do in August and September. Miller's words give purpose to those months. Being deliberate and explicit about the smallest of details is essential. If my students don't know what I expect of them, come January they are certainly not to blame when things are not going as planned. It takes a considerable amount of time, patience, and energy to be deliberate in those first several weeks though, especially when curriculum is impatiently piling up. Rushing into the academic fray too early without a sure foundation could sabotage everything. "Slow down to speed up" is my mantra. If I'm not mistaken, I made that up, but it was inspired by the following quotations:

Slow down and be consistent.

-Kathy Collins

Spending time on procedures and management in the beginning is, in fact, good teaching and a good time investment.

-Kathy Collins

We move slowly to eventually move fast. The payoff is enormous.
                                                    -Gail Boushey and Joan Moser

To move slowly at the beginning does not necessarily mean that by the end of the year I will have accomplished less. In fact, I believe quite the opposite is true. I'll be able to speed up and accomplish so much more because I'll likely have fewer management issues along the way, and those always slow things down. I would rather purposefully take things slowly in August than have to slow down later out of sheer desperation.

27. Excellent Teaching Trumps All

We feel so pressured with the limited time we do have that we may commit to instructional activities we don't truly value. We need to stop and reflect.

-Regie Routman

In honor of spring state testing, my first graders are asked to read an end-of-year passage to a total stranger who's holding a stopwatch. They have to read 53 words per minute or more in order to score at or above grade level.

During the weeks leading up to the test, I refuse to:

- ask my readers to read random, meaningless passages.
- let them see me with a stopwatch in my hand.
- talk to them about words per minute.
- tell them that they're going to be tested.

Instead I:

- continue on with balanced literacy instruction (shared reading, mini-lessons, independent reading, guided reading, etc.) using real, authentic literature.
- give them opportunities to practice fluency strategies with familiar rereads and favorite weekly poems.
- encourage them to read with a storyteller's voice, to put their words together like they're talking, and to scoop words together.
- say these words the morning of the test: "Hey kiddos. Some good friends of mine are going to check your smart parts today. They'll take great care of you. Just be brave and do your best."

In the face of the inevitable mandated test, I still believe in the power of excellent literacy instruction and quality literature. Passages and stopwatches squeeze the life right out of our readers. Some might argue that these tools prepare readers for a better testing experience. Even if that's the case, and I have my doubts, I'd rather prepare my readers for a better reading life.

In whatever testing season you might find yourself in, stop and reflect. Excellent teaching trumps all.

28. GRACE

Teachers teach what they know and expanding what teachers know produces a substantial impact on students.

-Richard Allington

I was doing my best when I gave identical spelling lists and tests to each child instead of letting their daily writing drive my spelling instruction. I was doing my best when I thought writers should only write one short piece during a writing workshop session instead of expecting them to start a new one as soon as they were done. I was doing my best when I provided all the math strategies to my mathematicians instead of allowing them to invent their own.

I could go on and on. Naturally over my twenty-three years of teaching, I've left a trail of constantly changing practices. As the sayings goes, when you know better, you do better. The main thing is that I was doing my best. I'm reminded to give myself a break when I think about the kind of education I provide my students now compared to twenty-three years ago or even five. I'm beyond grateful that I continually outgrow my current version of best.

I'm also reminded to give others a break. I will admit it's easy to be critical when I hear of certain practices occurring in classrooms that are not in the best interests of our students. In light of the growth I've experienced throughout my career, though, it would be wise to show others the same grace I've shown myself.

I often envision the teaching profession as a path without end. It's occupied by teachers but all at different points. They're all moving but at varying paces. Then I spot myself. It's plain to see how far I've come, and I can identify many teachers who are currently where I once was. They deserve my grace. I can also look ahead to where I'd like to be and see many teachers occupying that space. I hope they show me grace as well.

I know the moral of Allington's quote is that our students are impacted by our best. Wherever we happen to be on the path of this profession, our best must constantly become better. The more we know, the better off our students will be. And along the way, we can show grace both to ourselves and others.

29. I SEE YOU

Too many of our students — and colleagues, too — remain invisible to us. They are physically present but mostly silent.

-Regie Routman

In a school of over 1,000 teenagers it's easier to be lost than found, but the seniors in my cousin Laurie's AP senior Literature classes know she sees them. From day one, her message is, "I see you." This motto is even on the wall of her classroom. It's one thing to verbalize or even display but completely different to live out, and that's what she strives for on a daily basis.

Her practice challenges me to do better. Even though I have a fraction of the students she has, there are times when it feels like some of my little people are slipping through my fingers. There are no good excuses, yet I can be distracted by the clock in my head. Plus, honestly it's simply easier to see the strengths and personalities of some more than others. Then there are seasons when I'm in survival mode and can hardly see through the fog. For reasons such as these, it's possible to lose sight of the most important job I have in the classroom — seeing all of my students in all of their greatness.

For the past few years, I've taken on the challenge of finding and documenting for students and parents three beautiful things each day in my classroom. That equals over 500 pictures and descriptions shared on my class website in a year's time. And because I keep track of who I take pictures of, I know I've repeatedly found beautiful things showcasing all my students. This has forced me to see the silent ones who can be easily overlooked and to celebrate the ones who are desperate to be seen in a positive light. An added bonus is that they see each other, since each day a new student is responsible for finding three of their own beautiful things for our class website, which they take seriously. How about this one: "Lawrence doesn't give up even when it is hard."

Routman precedes the above quotation with this thought. "I'll never forget seeing the blockbuster movie *Avatar* and being struck that the word *love* was not in the Avatar culture. To express that emotion, a character would say, 'I see you' which translated to 'I know who you are,' 'I understand you,' 'I value you.'" My cousin Laurie sees her students. I've discovered my way. What's yours?

30. Expecting Ambiguity

The strongest predictors of learning are a strong desire to communicate, willingness to appear foolish, and a willingness to live with vagueness.
                                                            -Roberto Bahruth

I recall a time when I spent three days of summer acquainting myself with a document called the Common Core. At that point, it was not a way of life yet. Learning the ins and outs of the standards and what it all meant for my classroom was an enormous task, as educators across this nation know all too well. Throughout the early process of fumbling with the Common Core, I found myself recalling the words of Bahruth, a wise professor and author who taught one of my master's courses at Boise State University.

"Willingness to live with vagueness." That line in particular resonated with my Common Core experience. Vagueness can either be handled (or maybe mishandled) with stress and worry or with the knowledge that vagueness and learning are a package deal. I've learned over the years when diving into a new practice to allow myself time to figure it out as I go. In my experience, teachers tend to put themselves under too much pressure to know and master new practices on day one, when in reality it takes time to conquer change. Realistically, sometimes the vagueness lingers months into the process.

In actuality, we're practicing what we expect of our students, who, according to Bahruth, deal with vagueness rather naturally. Maybe we can take a tip from them and embrace the ambiguity. Whether it's Common Core, a new method for teaching math, experimenting with writing workshop, or myriad other new, innovative practices, let's not be surprised by the vagueness. Instead we can expect it, recognize it, deal with it, and know it won't remain forever. Ambiguity is not necessarily the enemy; it's a reminder to gift yourself with the time to learn something new.

31. THEIR LIVES MATTER

When we help children know that their lives do matter, we are teaching writing.

-Lucy Calkins

It was the middle of our persuasive letter writing unit. One of my writers had a strong opinion about the lack of Weird Al songs played at a local radio station, so he wrote a persuasive letter about this problem and we sent it off. Were we ever surprised when a box about the size of a first grader arrived at our classroom door. It was filled with treasures from the radio station, along with a promise to remedy the Weird Al issue. This young writer was a hero that day.

Pushing a topic and audience onto my writers would never have brought these rewarding results. Neither would my restrictions have impressed upon them the all-important lesson that their opinions matter. Their lives matters. All my writers learned this lesson that day, and it's one that applies to any genre.

Sometimes I wonder why teacher-given topics are so prevalent. Is fear a factor? *My students don't know what they're doing. They're not confident writers. They might flounder, so I'd better provide a scaffold.* Is it state testing? *My students must know how to write to a topic, because that's how they'll be tested.* Is it unexamined wallpaper? *We've always done it this way.* There are likely myriad reasons, but I'm unsure that any reason is reason enough to completely remove choice from their writing lives.

"Don't steal your neighbor's thinking power," is a line straight out of my classroom. In essence, I believe a diet consisting solely of writing topics steals our writers' thinking power. It handcuffs their opportunity to think — to struggle for that idea that might turn into something extraordinary, to value their own experiences and thoughts, to find that their lives really do matter.

When given the opportunity and support, even our youngest writers should experience the authentic struggle and accomplishment of writing about their own ideas and expressing them in creative ways. With the right guidance and practice, they'll even be able to write successfully on that random day when asked to write to a topic. Their lives do matter and choice within writing teaches them just that.

32. More Isn't Necessary

Kids learn to read by reading and write by writing. It sounds so simplistic that we often think we need to do more. Instead we miss the one thing we can truly give our students for relatively low cost: more time immersed in text.

-Susan Nations and Mellissa Alonso

Over ten years ago I made my first quilt. This was not a walk-in-the-park undertaking, considering I had never turned on a sewing machine. I managed to produce a quilt worth displaying in public, but I didn't learn to quilt by doing little sewing exercises on the side. I learned to quilt by quilting. I was immersed in the process from the very first cut and stitch and became a quilter the moment I took on the project.

Of course, sewing and literacy are different beasts, but the premise of learning a new craft is the same. As the quote says, kids learn to read by reading, and they learn to write by writing. It's easy to get caught up in the "more," which can take on many different faces. More activities, more games, more centers, more glorified worksheets, etc. which the internet has made quite easy for teachers to access. The "more" is what Debbie Diller, in *Literacy Work Stations*, challenges teachers to beware of when they look at lesson plans with a critical eye. She asks teachers to identify activities and methods that truly help students become better readers and writers, not things they hope will have this result.

Regie Routman refers to activities *about* reading and writing as "stuff." Stuff isn't necessarily evil and there are times when it serves a purpose, but it can so quickly push time for real reading and writing out the door. Time to be readers and writers is the best thing we can give our students that will make the biggest difference in their literacy. The "more" isn't necessary.

33. Borrow Wisely

We need to be gatekeepers for sane and sensible practices.

-Regie Routman

While my least favorite educational word is fidelity, my favorite is pedagogy. Although I likely pronounce its third syllable incorrectly, it feels like I'm talking about something special when I use that word.

Pedagogy is indeed a big deal. Methods and practices are a foundation for most everything a teacher does in the classroom, regardless of experience. Even our newest members to the profession have a pedagogy. In fact, they have one long before a stamp of approval lands on that teaching certificate.

So where does this pedagogy come from?

I devised my own hypothesis based on twenty-three years of teaching. Then I tried out my question on my nephew Kyle, who is in his first year of teaching, to see how our answers compared. In his response he referred to past teachers, college courses, and the excellent teachers who surround him. Basically, his answer confirmed what I'd been thinking all along.

We borrow pedagogy.

It might be an oversimplification, but I'm certain I borrowed pedagogy before I had my own classroom, and twenty-three years later, I'm still borrowing new practices and methods. Some I held on to way too long, like mad minutes and the public evidence of mastery posted on the wall. This was before I had developed the skill of being a gatekeeper — one who examines pedagogy with a critical eye and is unafraid to turn unsound practices away on behalf of the children in my care. We have a responsibility to help our new teachers develop this skill. Although I believe Kyle is already thinking like a gatekeeper, I hope our newest teachers don't tire of us reminding them to borrow wisely. It might be some of the best advice we can give.

34. COMMENTS OR QUESTIONS?

In problem solving, the three most important things are talk, talk, talk —
and the children should do most of the talking.

-Larry Buschman

I've spent the last five years making significant changes to the mathematical methods I use. Sometimes this process and the resulting outcome brings me great joy. And sometimes the opposite is true. Though change is slow and hard, there are moments when I realize I'm doing something right. Increasing student talk during problem solving-lessons is one of those moments.

One of my favorite math lessons involves sending students to the board who have worked out a solution to a problem in their math journals in ways I think everyone needs to see. In the olden days I took over as soon as the child drew his strategy on the board. I asked him questions and prompted accordingly while the class watched and hopefully listened. It was a step in the right direction, but it was missing something — less of me and more of him.

Now the child who is sharing is in charge from beginning to end. It might sound like this. Kellen describes his strategy and says, "Comments or questions?" As I stand back and listen, hands shoot into the air. "Leland?" Kellen calls out. "Why didn't you use tallies?" Leland asks. "It would have taken me too long," Kellen responds. Since Kellen is in charge he calls on more students, who typically ask insightful questions like the one Leland asked. Kellen is forced to think about why he made the choices he made and then find a way to communicate those reasons to the class. Even though I'm there to turn the conversation in ways I feel would be most beneficial, it's been good to step back and listen to the students do most of the talking.

I have a lot to learn about quality problem-solving instruction, but hearing kids do more talking about how math makes sense to them leads me to believe I'm on the right track. Comments or questions?

35. It Takes Guts

Much of your success as an educator has to do with your attitude towards teaching and towards kids. The rest of your success is based on your willingness to relentlessly search for what engages students in the classroom and then having the guts to do it.

-Dave Burgess

My cousin Laurie teaches AP senior literature. Imagine a class full of seniors in the midst of a Socratic Seminar discussion. While the inner circle of students is responsible for conversing out loud, the outer circle has out their phones or other electronic devices. They're responsible for tweeting about the discussion in the circle. As we all know, high schoolers are all about phones, devices, and social media. So imagine the buzz around this lesson.

Inviting this new method of engagement into her class is brilliant but took guts. Consider those who might not understand or might find themselves uncomfortable with such a bold move. It takes a shift in thinking to take Socratic Seminar this direction. Then there's the question of whether it would all turn out like she had imagined it in her head. She knew she likely wouldn't get it 100% right the first time. In spite of all this, I've no doubt having guts paid off.

I've personally and repeatedly found that it take guts to be a teacher. After independently pursuing a passionate topic or reading a professional book, my classroom becomes an experiment to discover how the ideas I pursued translate into my practice. It can be messy and scary, yet the pursuit of best practices and the guts to try them on for size has much to do with where I am today.

And it takes guts to go it alone, if need be. If my cousin Laurie had waited for others to find themselves mentally and physically ready to integrate Twitter into their lessons, she'd likely never experiment with such innovative techniques. That doesn't mean she doesn't share and collaborate, but taking risks means she's willing to make the leap, even if she's the only one.

Countless times I've done my own searching for best practices and then thrown myself into a possible lion's den, regardless of what anyone else was doing. In those moments there is no waiting for others, and I've never felt comfortable pushing anyone into my version of a deep end. My passionate topic or practice might not be theirs, yet. I do believe it's important to share and collaborate, but I also believe in having the guts to blaze the trail. Sometimes that's all others need in order to make a similar leap of their own.

When it comes to our students and what engages them, we might not always get it right the first or even the second time, and we might be alone in the experimentation process, but having the guts to try what we feel is best for kids can create a buzz amongst our students that will bring them back for more. That makes having guts worthwhile.

36. Learn, Not Pay

*Kids want to know they matter to you. They want to know you see them,
hear them, and believe in them — unconditionally.*
                          -Todd Nesloney and Adam Welcome

Due to my involvement in The Idaho Coaching Network, I've missed several
days of school in the last year. I can count on one hand the number of sick
days I've had in twenty-three years of teaching, so being gone once a month is
atypical and extremely difficult on me.

   I shake my head when I think about what my students will or won't do in
my absence. If I were a fly on the wall, I know I'd be disappointed. Maybe
that's my ever-present control freak nature. Maybe it's because I teach my
students that character is doing what's right even when no one is watching.
Likely it's both. Either way, I returned from my most recent absence to hear
that the guest teacher and my class had a rough day.

   Honestly, the news was immensely frustrating and even hurtful. I'll admit
I took it personally. I wanted to apologize on behalf of my people. Yeah,
they're only six or seven and far from perfect, but they know better. Doing
the right thing when Miss McMorrow isn't watching is not always easy but it's
important. (They hear this from me often.) In the early stages of my
frustration, growth mindset wasn't on my mind. Yet I came around.

   While scrapping my original plans for the following day and wondering
how I was going to fix a moment gone bad, I found inspiration and direction
in words that magically and unexpectedly overtook my disheartened thoughts.

I don't want them to pay. I want them to learn.

I don't believe I've ever specifically thought about this before, and I mourned for the times when I've subconsciously led with a you-will-pay-for-this mindset. I don't recall ever intentionally doing this, but at some point in my career, I've no doubt had a moment, or several, when paying took priority over learning — or paying was disguised as learning. It's so easy to unintentionally slip into this mode.

So I went into the day with a plan — a plan for them to learn, not pay. Every conversation and activity sent a clear message about who we want to be, intertwined with these and other similar words: "Remember on the first day of school when I said I loved you before you even showed up? That's still true and nothing can change that."

37. Outstanding

Nothing was as powerful as the quality of the teacher in predicting the achievement of children.

-Richard Allington

"What are the qualities of an outstanding teacher?" When my principal asked a prospective new teacher this question, I couldn't help but create my own list. Although likely incomplete, I aspire to be this teacher on a daily basis:

- An outstanding teacher inspires. She doesn't simply convey information. She grows greatness in each student academically, socially, and personally.

- An outstanding teacher has great classroom management. The culture and atmosphere of her classroom environment allows for more learning and less managing.

- An outstanding teacher is organized. There are so many balls to juggle as a teacher. Disorganization has the potential to interfere with student learning.

- An outstanding teacher constantly reflects. She can verbalize what she can improve upon, as well as what she's doing well. She also knows why she's doing what she's doing.

- An outstanding teacher is a gatekeeper. She stands at the door of her classroom and protects her students from unhealthy practices. She doesn't allow an idea passage simply because everyone else is doing it.

- An outstanding teacher never stops growing. She doesn't allow herself the satisfaction of thinking she knows it all. She pursues her own professional development.

- An outstanding teacher has high expectations. She knows what her students have the potential to do both academically and behaviorally and teaches them from day one the habits of reaching those expectations.

- An outstanding teacher strives for real-world instruction. There's authenticity, meaning, and purpose to what she asks of her students.

Again, what are the qualities of an outstanding teacher? It's a perfect question to ask possible new additions to a school staff, especially considering the correlation between teacher quality and student achievement. It's also a great question to ponder as someone who's been in the profession for over twenty years. There are days, weeks, and sometimes months when being outstanding seems like a lofty goal, but these qualities remind me that several little people are counting on me to strive to be at the top of my game at all times.

38. MY PROMISE

When a child enters your school, what is the promise that you make to the child and her parents about the writing education that she will receive?

-Lucy Calkins

I remember my first encounter with this quote. My school's instructional coach asked the staff to carefully ponder Calkins' question and create a Writing Bill of Rights, so to speak. Since then, I've repeatedly returned to this plea of Calkins' to intentionally think about the promises we should make to our writers and their parents. In fact, I've found it to be such a pivotal and forgotten question that I've asked several teachers to consider it when I've led professional development. What an important conversation to have as an individual and as a school. The values and beliefs we have about writing tend to float to the surface when we draft the promises we'd like to make. The discussion has the potential to create enlightening shifts in our thinking and practices. I don't want to influence your possible promises, but I can't help but share mine.

I promise that . . .

- There will be a structure or plan to your child's writing time. It will begin with a mini-lesson, followed by time to write, and finished with an opportunity to share and celebrate what's going well.

- Every mini-lesson will teach him something he can try in his writing that day.

- I will give your child feedback. I will acknowledge what he's doing well and nudge him to try something that will hopefully improve him as a writer, not just improve the piece he's currently working on.

- Your child will be constantly writing during writing time. There will be no waiting for me to read everything he writes. When he finishes one piece, he'll start another.

- Your child will write for a variety of authentic audiences.

- Your child will choose his own writing topics.

- Your child will frequently see me model the writing process. He will also share the writing process with me as the class writes together.

- Your child will study the work of mentor authors.

- Your child will experience writing a variety of genres.

- Your child will have many opportunities throughout the day to write.

- Your child's use of conventions and spelling is important, but his ideas and content will be valued first.

What is your promise?

39. Engaged or On-Task?

Make sure students are engaged, not just on-task.

-Regie Routman

A friend of mine works in a position where she has random opportunities to make brief appearances in classrooms. She gets at-a-glance views of various teachers and students at work. Recently she was telling me about a teacher whose students always seem to be busy working when she drops in. She used the word "engaged." I asked, "Are they engaged or are they on task?" There is a vast difference.

Of course, I can't ask that question about another teacher without asking the same about my students. Simply because they are occupied and rarely wasting a minute does not mean they are engaged in what they're doing. They could be going through the motions, and if that's the case, I'm wasting their time.

I believe engagement happens when students find purpose and meaning in tasks. If the work is authentic and founded on the interests of their own world, they are more likely to put their hearts into it. Engagement is also more likely to occur when tasks are not too easy or too hard. Both extremes are off-putting and difficult to embrace.

Some might call this flow. I've experienced it in my room. It has a magical, satisfying feel to it. I felt the magic when I showed my students The Kid President's video, *20 Things We Should Say More Often*, put them into small groups, and asked them to brainstorm their own lists of words we should say more often. They chose their top 10 and created colorful posters to present to another classroom, as well as post throughout our school. That whole experience was magical. But I've also experienced what the untrained eye might believe is flow but is actually a classroom of compliant students who are simply on task. It's all a masquerade. So how we do convert those on-task moments into ones where students are completely engaged?

Day after day and lesson after lesson, I want to consistently challenge myself to dissect what I'm asking of my students. Will this engage them or will it keep them on task? The latter just isn't good enough.

40. Immerse Yourself

The secret to becoming a better teacher is total immersion. Your ability to completely give yourself up to the moment and fully "be" with your students is an awesome and unmistakably powerful technique.
                                                                -Dave Burgess

In my everyday life, I'm married to routines and plans, but in my travels to Europe, I expect exploration and immersion, even the kind that leads to moments of wondering where I am. One summer I went on a Mediterranean cruise with my parents. Our stop at the Greek island of Mykonos was not nearly long enough. All I really desired was to lose myself in the maze of circuitous narrow walkways encompassed by whitewashed stone buildings, adorned with a rainbow of brightly painted doors and shutters. That would have made for the perfect visit. We simply weren't given enough time for the kind of immersion into the Mykonos life that I yearned for.

Back in my world of teaching, there are very few lost minutes in my room. I teach with a sense of urgency, as Regie Routman recommends. I believe in the benefits of routine and sticking to the well-marked path. I know where we need to go and how to get us there. I also recognize the dangers. When a fork in the road presents itself, which is more important? My plans or my students?

At the beginning of one school year I found myself repeating some of the words from Burgess' quote above. "Just be. Immerse yourself. If something comes up that's not part of your original plan, just go with it." Although I celebrated some moments of immersion, I also missed the mark one day. Two of my boys requested I read a third David Shannon book, but all I could see were my plans and the clock. I had a list of reasons why following their lead honestly wasn't ideal. And there was my fork in the road. Considering how passionate I am about literacy, I took the wrong way.

I eventually backtracked and found that third David Shannon book to read. I also reminded myself, "Expect exploration and immersion, even the kind that leads to moments of being lost." Amidst routines and plans that I still believe are essential, I must remember that sometimes losing oneself is the most memorable part of the visit.

41. LIVING IT

Teachers who read for pleasure are more likely to employ best literacy practices in their classrooms than teachers who do not read for pleasure.
                                                            -Donalyn Miller

A friend once told me a story about an acquaintance of hers who is a running coach. I couldn't believe it when she told me the coach hates to run. I immediately thought, "First off, why in the world is she a running coach? Secondly, why would anyone choose her as a running coach?" I want the coach who can not only teach me about technique but who can and will inspire me. Great form is essential, but function, purpose, and the knowledge of why I should choose running over everything else is what makes the form worth working on. How can the coach inspire if she doesn't enjoy the act herself?

As a teacher of reading, I remind myself to teach with my own reading in mind. When I appreciate and acknowledge what reading does for my life, I can more easily transfer that knowledge into my classroom practice with my own readers. Without a real love for reading, I'm left to teach reading solely based on knowledge of phonics and sight words. That's not going to win anyone over.

My reading life creates purpose and intentionality, and it's why I throw my weight into the role of being a reading salesman. It's why I've ramped up my daily read-aloud minutes. It's why I fill my bag with irresistible library books every few weeks. It's why there was a large box sitting in my room on the first day of school with a sign attached stating, "Do Not Open (until Friday)." Talk about anticipation. Friday's big reveal established the fact that, in Miss McMorrow's room, a box full of books is a surprise worth waiting for.

What are the habits of real readers? Those are the authentic practices that must become the heart and soul of my reading curriculum, teaching my students the how of reading but, more importantly, inspiring them to become readers themselves. Students who catch that vision will know that reading is something worth doing for a lifetime. It's hard for them to be inspired by someone who doesn't personally live that reality themselves.

42. The 3 R's of Teaching

Unless teachers are encouraged to take time for reading, risking, and reflecting, no meaningful change will occur.

-Regie Routman

Simply put, reading + risking + reflecting = meaningful change. I suppose we could call them the 3 R's of teaching. Is this equation evident in our schools or, better yet, in our own classrooms?

Reading - Routman is fully aware of the busy lives we teachers live, but she also knows that books provide an invaluable kind of professional development that should find its way into our habits of being. The professional books on my shelves and in the piles on my living room floor are significant contributors to my teaching pedagogy. They've added greatly to the teacher I am now and the one I hope to be in ten years.

Risking - On a personal level, I'm not a risk-taker. As a teacher, I've learned that playing it safe is detrimental to my professional development, as well as to the growth of the learners in my care. When I take risks, I give myself permission to start something new without having all the answers first. Launching a Makerspace in my room this year is a perfect example. With a solid idea of why, but only a general idea of how, I found some of the answers I needed by jumping right in. Quality student learning time would have been wasted otherwise. I typically discover that my kids can handle a whole lot more than I ever give them credit for. They benefit from my risk-taking.

Reflecting - I must be willing to ask myself the hard questions even about the practices I most strongly believe in. Why? What's best for kids? What's best for this student? There are myriad questions that I can and should ask myself regardless of how long I've been doing this job. When it comes to teacher excellence and student success, I can't afford to leave any stone unturned.

Meaningful Change - We've probably all experienced the kind of change that essentially leads nowhere. The pendulum swings and schools, districts, and states react — sometimes unwisely. How often have you found yourself asking, "Now, *why* are we doing this?" Those changes are most often out of our control. In my experience, the most meaningful change happens when I take professional development into my own hands.

I'm rarely satisfied with the teacher I am today, but I'm the only one who can change that. I read. I risk. I reflect. If Routman is right, and I think she is, that means I'm bound to change in meaningful ways.

43. NO GUILT

*No single literacy activity has a more positive effect on students'
comprehension, vocabulary knowledge, spelling, writing ability, and
overall academic achievement than free voluntary reading.*
-Donalyn Miller

There aren't many times in the day when my kids have to wonder, "What do I
do now?" If they complete a piece of writing during writing workshop, they
start a new one. If they finish a book during read to self, they read another. In
those rare moments when there is a task that they'll finish at different times
and need something to do upon completion, they learn quickly to find a book
in our room and a place to read.

Many teachers have fancy systems in place for students who finish tasks
early. Pinterest and Teachers Pay Teachers are full of them. Even though I've
believed in my simple system of providing kids with more time with books,
once upon a time I would have felt slightly guilty about this.

When I finished *The Book Whisperer*, I had to thank Donalyn Miller for
validating my read-when-you're-finished plan. She makes it plain that kids
must spend more time with their noses in books. Reading trumps all other
activities, and she talks about the ways she squeezes out as much extra reading
time in her day as she possibly can. Richard Allington is also known for
beseeching teachers to increase the volume of daily in-school reading. Adding
to the conversation is Regie Routman who says, "We no longer need to feel
guilty that students are 'just reading.' Reading is probably the most worthwhile
activity students can be doing." Needless to say, I no longer feel an iota of
guilt when my readers head off to various parts of the room with books in
tow. Any way I can get books into their hands is not only okay, it's essential.

44. REFLECTIVE AND EFFECTIVE

We must be willing to look with fresh eyes at what we do and ask, "Is there a better way?"

-George Couros

My cousin Kevin, assistant principal and educator extraordinaire, asks the following question when interviewing at his school. *What is the most important quality of an effective teacher?* His favorite answer is "reflective." A reflective teacher is unlikely to lose her effectiveness because she asks the right questions to that "better way." Our conversation about this particular teacher quality and my recent summer reads inspired me to venture into the new year with four reflective questions on my radar.

Why?
I can't help but think of the unexamined wallpaper that Donalyn Miller challenges teachers to think about in *The Book Whisperer.* No matter where the practice originated, whether I was taught that way, a mentor teacher suggested it, it came from across the hall, or it's the way I've always done it, I must ask "Why?" If the answer doesn't align with what's best for the children, then the wallpaper is outdated and in need of removal.

What if?
This question hasn't been part of my reflective repertoire before, but I love the possibilities it offers for students and for teachers. It challenges me to think outside of my comfort zone and perceived limitations.

What's best for kids?

It's really the bottom line isn't it? It's why we all do what we do day in and day out. Todd Nesloney and Adam Welcome remind us in *Kids Deserve It!* that "Schools don't exist so adults can have jobs. Schools exist for students." It seems like the most obvious statement ever, but if I truly believe it, then my daily practice had better prove so.

What is best for *this* kid?
This question obviously takes the previous one to the next level. I must remember that every child deserves to have this question answered on his or her behalf. There's no giving up on anyone.

There's such a varied number of questions we teachers could be asking ourselves. Whether I've listed your favorites or not isn't necessarily the point. The point is be effective by being reflective. Our kids deserve our best, and we must continually seek it. What do you need to ask yourself?

45. Long Obedience

Learning to teach is an ongoing process and I know that I'll never really "get there."

-Carol Avery

I want to perfect first grade. This has been a career goal of mine since day one. Yet Avery reminds me I'll never get there, and I'm okay with that. Never reaching perfection doesn't deter me. On the contrary, it gives me energy. It's my drive. Donalyn Miller's analogy from *Reading in the Wild* explains it so well:

"My friend Jim who lives in San Francisco told me that maintenance workers continuously paint the Golden Gate Bridge. Workers paint as well as they can as far as they can every day, accepting any conditions that affect their progress such as the fog, which limits the number of hours in a day they can paint. When they are done painting in one area, they start on another. The crew never really finishes the job; they just continue."

My teaching career is the Golden Gate Bridge. It's been a giant undertaking. I'm not sure what I would have thought twenty-four years ago if I had completely understood what I was up against. What would I have done if instead of a ceremony and diploma, I'd been metaphorically plopped down in front of the Golden Gate Bridge and told, "Your career will be like this bridge. Here's your paintbrush. Now start painting." I probably would have said, "You're kidding me, right?" Even now after years of experience, from where I currently stand on this bridge, I can hardly see to the other side and to what's awaiting me there. Admittedly at moments I feel overwhelmed when I look up to catch a glimpse of how much I still have left to accomplish. It can be both intimidating and thrilling at the same time. To complicate matters, the conditions that affect my progress are many, unpredictable, and often out of my control. In spite of the daily problems that impede progress, like the Golden Gate Bridge, this journey is a beautiful thing, partly as a result of the determination it requires to pick up that brush day after day, knowing there's never a moment of completion. My Uncle Burt would call it, "Long obedience in the same direction."

46. Efficiency

Highly effective educators are highly efficient.

-Regie Routman

I have my share of teacher pet peeves. One of my favorites is the amount of time it takes for teachers to walk out the door when the recess bell rings. I believe the bell signals the end of my time and the start of my students', so I'm out the door the second I hear it. (Not to mention, nothing ever good happens in an unattended line of youngsters.) A few years ago, a brand new teacher spent a day in my classroom and noted my recess bell procedure. She did the math and estimated that I saved a total of twenty instructional minutes by my efficient routine.

Efficient means "achieving maximum productivity with minimum wasted effort or expense." Routman's quote prodded me to consider my day and the things I have in place that make my practice efficient. My list is not exhaustive, but everything here plays an essential part in the efficiency of the classroom and success of students.

- Start establishing systems on day one. Assume nothing. Consistently model and have students repeatedly practice routines and procedures from how to stand in line to how they move around the room.

- Good classroom management is a priority. Efficiency is hard to achieve in the midst of chaos, consistent interruptions, or distracting off-task behavior. High expectations help streamline a variety of classroom systems and minimize wasteful by-products.

- Pacing is important not only within a lesson but from one lesson to the next. Downtime is dangerous. Plan for educational and fun transitions and breaks.

- Instruction should be authentic and purposeful. Students are much more productive when they care about and see a purpose for what they are doing. Busywork doesn't cut it.

- Organization is a priority. Time is wasted when materials are not where they're supposed to be, if there is no system for collecting, organizing, and working with student information, or if the day-to-day long to-do list cannot be corralled.

Certainly there are moments, days, or weeks that are less efficient than others, but I believe Routman is still right. The more efficient I am, the more effective I will be, and my students will reap the benefits.

47. The Business of Selling

I believe great teaching incorporates many of the same skills and techniques used in successful salesmanship and marketing.

-Dave Burgess

I would make a horrible salesman. I imagine feelings of guilt with every sale. Yet I've realized over the years that I really am in sales. I did not recognize this facet of my career in my early years of teaching, but I've come to see it as a vital part of my classroom practice. In fact, the beginning of the year is one big sales pitch in my room.

"Did you know that Mr. Graves sends me the best kids in the **whole** school?"

"You're full of greatness."

"I loved you before you even showed up."

"I'm so glad you're all can-doers. I know none of you would dream of throwing your pencil on the floor, crossing your arms, and crying like a baby when something is hard."

"Mrs. Palmer, it is your lucky day. The **best** kids in the school have finally arrived. You're the luckiest librarian on the planet."

"I know you all love it when you get to work on another challenging math problem."

"Reading is one of my all-time favorite things to do. Have I mentioned that I love to read? I don't know if I told you this before, but I really love to read."

"I chose this book because I know how much you all love to read."

"I hate to do this to you because I know you all love to write so much, but it's time to put away your writing tools."

Reading the Burgess quote and making this list heightened my awareness of the ways I sell my product. More importantly, it sparked a conscious need for other sales avenues in my practice. What part of my product line needs better promotion? How can I sell these products even more successfully? Simply put, I'm in the business of selling, and learning is the most important product any of these kids will ever invest in.

48. Expect Nothing in Return

I have never observed a student who developed a long-term reading habit because of an incentive program.

-Donalyn Miller

Here's a little moment of truth from my own teaching experience, and I shudder to think that I did this. During my first few years of teaching there was a chart on the back wall of my classroom listing every child's name. I used it to tally the number of books each one read at home. Every time a child read ten books, she earned some kind of trinket, which was most likely soon lost, broken, or forgotten.

The whole situation makes me cringe. First off, any kind of public display of "progress" is dangerous in my opinion, whether we're communicating about reading, behavior, homework, or math fact fluency. It would be inappropriate to walk into the teachers' lounge and see Miss McMorrow's test scores, whether good or bad, on the wall. Student experience is no different. I'm embarrassed for those who had only a few tallies, especially considering the fact that for the most part, at my grade level, nightly reading is a parental issue. Secondly, rewarding students for reading is the wrong message. Reading *is* the reward.

As much as possible, school reading and life reading should be one and the same, yet how often is that not the case? As an adult reader, no one rewards me after I read ten books. My reward is so much meaningful, and that's the experience we must give our readers. Their reward should be found in the ways their hearts, minds, and lives connect with the books they read and the other readers who enjoy those same books. What if our readers didn't know about reading incentives? What if they just knew how wonderful it feels to be readers? That's my goal for every student in my room, and my sincere hope is that those whose names were on that back wall somehow learned to love reading in spite of all the ways I once did it wrong.

49. LISTEN TO YOUR HEART

Teach to the heart as well as the head.

-Roberto Bahruth

A small turquoise wooden frame sits on a shelf in the library of my classroom. Stitched into the fabric inside are the words "Listen to your heart," along with three stitched hearts. It's obvious the same first-grade hand lovingly and carefully stitched every stroke. In fact, there's proof in the bottom right-hand corner where the creator left her initials — J.M. This frame might be the best student gift I've received, because I love when my words echo back to me from the voices of my students. It feels like the highest compliment.

To my knowledge Bahruth is not famous throughout the world, but he is brilliant, and he taught me a few things while I was earning my master's degree ten years ago. I don't recall many specifics about his class, Psycholinguistics and Reading, but I do distinctly remember, "Teach to the heart as well as the head."

What will my students remember about my class ten years from now? Will they remember all the reading, writing, and math we did? There's certainly nothing wrong with remembering those things, since first graders blossom a great deal in all those areas. More than anything, my hope is that they remember, "Listen to your heart." It has become one of my favorite classroom mantras. It often sounds like this: "Listen to your heart. It will never let you down. Would it *ever* tell you to refuse to give someone's spot back? Would it tell you to run in the hallway?" This conversation is often accompanied by a little tapping on my chest and sometimes, in those one-on-one moments, a light tapping on a student's as well.

I pray I've given all my students the practice to have ears to hear and the desire to listen for what their hearts are truly saying. Maybe this is pie in the sky, but ten years from now when one of my students is in a sticky situation, I pray she can hear Miss McMorrow's voice and feel the warmth of my hand on her chest. "Listen to your heart."

Thank you, J.M., for reminding me to continue teaching to the heart as well as the head.

50. Surrounded by Greatness

Do whatever we can to first capture students'... hearts before worrying about how much we are teaching them.

-Regie Routman

When my new crew arrived on the first day of school, I looked at all their faces, borrowed a line from my pastor, and with arms open wide said, "I'm surrounded by greatness." Even with an accompanying first-grade friendly explanation, their collective blank looks were proof that my words sailed over most of their heads. Yet I persistently returned to this refrain, let it repeatedly sink in, and before long it naturally morphed into, "You're full of greatness." A new mantra was born. These same students on that first day of school also heard me passionately declare, "I loved you before you even showed up." My students heard affirmations about love and greatness before I had an inkling about attitudes, temperaments, or abilities. They did nothing to earn any of these declarations, but their names were on my roster. That's all it took.

Words have creative power, and I believe it's my job and honor to intentionally speak only the best ones into the atmosphere of my classroom and more specifically into each heart. It is possible my words will jumpstart a culture of respect, trust, and love. That's the kind of foundation every learning environment deserves.

I also believe I have a responsibility to influence the self-talk of my students. My voice goes with them, but it isn't the only voice my students hear in their heads. Their own voices matter and are naturally louder than my own. So imagine a class of first graders saying The Pledge of Allegiance each morning. "...One nation under God, indivisible with liberty and justice for all. I am *full* of greatness." That's what you would hear in my room, and that's what I hope my students hear in their heads every time they say the pledge, long after they leave first grade.

It would be dishonest and unreasonable to imply that I see evidence of this greatness in all students in all moments, or that it's easy to be that loving teacher I professed to be on the first day of school, when I'm shedding tears of frustration a month later. I admit that distracting behaviors sometimes prevent me from seeing their greatness. As their teacher, I owe it to them to give it my best, though. Their greatness is non-negotiable, and they deserve to know it.

REFERENCES

Introduction
Goldberg, N. (2005). *Writing down the bones: Freeing the writer within*. Boston, MA: Shambhala.
Routman, R. (2008). *Teaching essentials: Expecting the most and getting the best from every learner, K-8*. Portsmouth, NH: Heinemann.

1. I Am the Teacher
Burgess, D. (2012). *Teach like a pirate: Increase student engagement, boost your creativity, and transform your life as an educator*. San Diego, CA: Dave Burgess Consulting, Inc.

2. Be a Gas Station
Graves, D. H. (1994). *A fresh look at writing*. Portsmouth, NH: Heinemann.

3. A Lot of Easy
Routman, R. (1994). *Invitations: Changing as teachers and learners K-12*. Portsmouth, NH: Heinemann.
Sullivan, J. (1996, September). Personal interview.

4. Unexamined Wallpaper
Miller, D. (2011). *The book whisperer: Awakening the inner reader in every child*. New York, NY: Scholastic.

5. Lessons Gone Bad
Diller, D. (2003). *Literacy work stations: Making centers work*. Portland, ME: Stenhouse Publishers.
Routman, R. (2008). *Teaching essentials: Expecting the most and getting the best from every learner, K-8*. Portsmouth, NH: Heinemann.

6. Cut Some Strings
Miller, D. (2011). *The book whisperer: Awakening the inner reader in every child*. New York, NY: Scholastic.

7. Expect More
Routman, R. (2005). *Writing essentials: Raising expectations and results while simplifying teaching*. Portsmouth, NH: Heinemann.

8. Answers Solve Nothing
Buschman, L. (2003). *Share and compare: A teacher's story about helping children become problem solvers in mathematics.* Reston, VA: NCTM.

9. It's Not Always Easy
Hertz, C., & Mraz, K. (2015). *A mindset for learning: Teaching the traits of joyful, independent growth.* Portsmouth, NH: Heinemann.

10. At My Fingertips
Couros, G. (2015). *The innovator's mindset: Empower learning, unleash talent, and lead a culture of creativity.* San Diego, CA: Dave Burgess Consulting, Inc.

11. Breaking the Code
Gentry. R. J. (2006). *Breaking the code: The new science of beginning reading.* Portsmouth, NH: Heinemann.

12. Two Kinds
Routman, R. (1996). *Literacy at the crossroads: Crucial talk about reading, writing, and other teaching dilemmas.* Portsmouth, NH: Heinemann.

13. The Practice of Mathematics
Fosnot, C.T., & Dolk, M. (2001). *Young mathematicians at work: Constructing number sense, addition, and subtraction.* Portsmouth, NH: Heinemann.

14. Start There
Routman, R. (2008). *Teaching essentials: Expecting the most and getting the best from every learner, K-8.* Portsmouth, NH: Heinemann.

15. Less Parent-Dependant
Allington, R. L. (2000). *What really matters for struggling readers: Designing research-based programs.* New York, NY: Addison-Wesley Educational Publishers Inc.

16. Cool to Ask Questions
Routman, R. (2008). *Teaching essentials: Expecting the most and getting the best from every learner, K-8.* Portsmouth, NH: Heinemann.

17. No Secrets
Graves. D. H. (1994). *A fresh look at writing.* Portsmouth, NH: Heinemann.

18. Failure or Feedback?
Burgess, D. (2012). *Teach like a pirate: Increase student engagement, boost your creativity, and transform your life as an educator.* San Diego, CA: Dave Burgess Consulting, Inc.

19. Just Because it Works
Burgess, D. (2012). *Teach like a pirate: Increase student engagement, boost your creativity, and transform your life as an educator.* San Diego, CA: Dave Burgess Consulting, Inc.

20. Rigor – Use Caution
Burgess, D. (2012). *Teach like a pirate: Increase student engagement, boost your creativity, and transform your life as an educator.* San Diego, CA: Dave Burgess Consulting, Inc.

21. A Little Messy
Taylor, S.P. (2008). *A quick guide to teaching persuasive writing, K-2.* Portsmouth, NH: Heinemann.

22. Beat Me to the Punch
Buschman, L. (2003). *Share and compare: A teacher's story about helping children become problem solvers in mathematics.* Reston, VA: NCTM.

23. Avoid the Pitfall
Routman, R. (2005). *Writing essentials: Raising expectations and results while simplifying teaching.* Portsmouth, NH: Heinemann.

24. Job Number 1
Allington, R. L. (2000). *What really matters for struggling readers: Designing research-based programs.* New York, NY: Addison-Wesley Educational Publishers Inc.

25. An Empty Room
Burgess, D. (2012). *Teach like a pirate: Increase student engagement, boost your creativity, and transform your life as an educator.* San Diego, CA: Dave Burgess Consulting, Inc.

26. Slow Down to Speed Up
Boushey, G., & Moser, J. (2006). *The daily 5: Fostering literacy independence in the elementary grades.* Portland, ME: Stenhouse.
Collins, C. (2004). *Growing readers: Units of study in the primary classroom.* Portland, ME: Stenhouse.

Diller, M. (2002). *Teaching with meaning: Teaching comprehension in the primary grades*. Portland, ME: Stenhouse.

27. Excellent Teaching Trumps All
Routman, R. (2005). *Writing essentials: Raising expectations and results while simplifying teaching*. Portsmouth, NH: Heinemann.

28. Grace
Allington, R. L. (2000). *What really matters for struggling readers: Designing research-based programs*. New York, NY: Addison-Wesley Educational Publishers Inc.

29. I See You
Routman, R. (2012). *Literacy and learning lessons from a longtime teacher*. Newark, DE: International Reading Association.

30. Expecting Ambiguity
Bahruth, R. (2002). Personal interview.

31. Their Lives Matter
Calkins, L. (1994). *The art of teaching writing*. Portsmouth, NH: Heinemann.

32. More Isn't Necessary
Diller, D. (2003). *Literacy work stations: Making centers work*. Portland, ME: Stenhouse. Publishers.
Nations, S., & Alonso, M. (2001). *Primary literacy centers: Making reading and writing stick*. Gainesville, FL: Maupin House.
Routman, R. (2002). Reading Essentials Workshop.

33. Borrow Wisely
Routman, R. (2008). *Teaching essentials: Expecting the most and getting the best from every learner, K-8*. Portsmouth, NH: Heinemann.

34. Comments or Questions?
Buschman, L. (2003). *Share and compare: A teacher's story about helping children become problem solvers in mathematics*. Reston, VA: NCTM.

35. It Takes Guts
Burgess, D. (2012). *Teach like a pirate: Increase student engagement, boost your creativity, and transform your life as an educator*. San Diego, CA: Dave Burgess Consulting, Inc.

36. Learn, Not Pay
Nesloney, T., & Welcome, A. (2016). *Kids deserve it: Pushing boundaries and challenging conventional thinking*. San Diego, CA: Dave Burgess Consulting, Inc.

37. Outstanding
Allington, R. L. (2000). *What really matters for struggling readers: Designing research-based programs*. New York, NY: Addison-Wesley Educational Publishers Inc.

38. My Promise
Calkins, L. (2013). *A guide to the common core writing workshop - primary grades*. Portsmouth, NH: Heinemann.

39. Engaged or On-Task?
Routman, R. (2012). *Literacy and learning lessons from a longtime teacher*. Newark, DE: International Reading Association.
"Kid President's 20 Things We Should Say More." *Youtube*, uploaded by SoulPancake, 21 November 2013, https://www.youtube.com/watch?v=m5yCOSHeYn4.

40. Immerse Yourself
Burgess, D. (2012). *Teach like a pirate: Increase student engagement, boost your creativity, and transform your life as an educator*. San Diego, CA: Dave Burgess Consulting, Inc.
Routman, R. (2003). *Reading essentials: The specifics you need to teach reading well*. Portsmouth, NH: Heinemann.
Shannon, D. (1998). *No, David!* New York, NY: The Blue Sky Press.
Shannon, D. (1999). *David goes to school*. New York, NY: The Blue Sky Press.
Shannon, D. (2002). *David gets in trouble*. New York, NY: The Blue Sky Press.

41. Living It
Miller, D. & Kelley, S. (2014). *Reading in the wild: The book whisperer's keys to cultivating lifelong reading habits*. San Francisco, CA: Jossey-Bass.

42. The Three R's of Teaching
Routman, R. (1994). *Invitations: Changing as teachers and learners K-12*. Portsmouth, NH: Heinemann.

43. No Guilt

Allington, R. L. (2000). *What really matters for struggling readers: Designing research-based programs.* New York, NY: Addison-Wesley Educational Publishers Inc.

Miller, D. (2011). *The book whisperer: Awakening the inner reader in every child.* New York, NY: Scholastic.

Routman, R. (1994). *Invitations: Changing as teachers and learners K-12.* Portsmouth, NH: Heinemann.

44. Reflective and Effective

Couros, G. (2015). *The innovator's mindset: Empower learning, unleash talent, and lead a culture of creativity.* San Diego, CA: Dave Burgess Consulting, Inc.

Miller, D. (2011). *The book whisperer: Awakening the inner reader in every child.* New York, NY: Scholastic.

Nesloney, T., & Welcome, A. (2016). *Kids deserve it: Pushing boundaries and challenging conventional thinking.* San Diego, CA: Dave Burgess Consulting, Inc.

45. Long Obedience

Avery, C. (1993). *And with a light touch: Learning about reading, writing, and teaching with first graders.* Portsmouth, NH: Heinemann.

Miller, D. & Kelley, S. (2014). *Reading in the wild: The book whisperer's keys to cultivating lifelong reading habits.* San Francisco, CA: Jossey-Bass.

46. Efficiency

Routman, R. (2012). *Literacy and learning lessons from a longtime teacher.* Newark, DE: International Reading Association.

47. The Business of Selling

Burgess, D. (2012). *Teach like a pirate: Increase student engagement, boost your creativity, and transform your life as an educator.* San Diego, CA: Dave Burgess Consulting, Inc.

48. Expect Nothing in Return

Miller, D. (2011). *The book whisperer: Awakening the inner reader in every child.* New York, NY: Scholastic.

49. Listen to Your Heart

Bahruth, R. (2002). Personal interview.

50. Surrounded by Greatness

Routman, R. (2012). *Literacy and learning lessons from a longtime teacher.* Newark, DE: International Reading Association.

ACKNOWLEDGMENTS

This book has been a long time coming, even before I knew it was such a thing, which means there are so many people who have had a hand in this project and deserve more than the few words I have space to give them. I hope they all know how honored I am to say thank you.

To my elementary teachers who loved my chubby cheeks and started this whole thing. Your love and care inspired me to be this teacher-leader I've become. Thank you for planting a seed.

To the Kuna School District for allowing me to be a gatekeeper. You trust me to make decisions based on what I believe is best for my students. Thank you for allowing me to be a professional.

To my blogging teacher friends who tolerate my soap boxes. You've been my listeners and my sounding board. Thank you for faithfully reading and commenting.

To my educator family members who don't mind talking about school 24/7, even on a Sunday morning at church. You challenge me to think outside my box, yet keep me centered on what's most important. Thank you for being my iron.

To Laur, Paula, and Jonelle who spent hours with all my words. You make me sound smarter than I am. Thank you for believing I have something worth saying.

To Jim who fanned the flame four years ago and has continued to support my dream. Thank you for adding your brilliance to my book.

To my family who thinks I'm the best first grade teacher in the world. You've loyally brought me flowers on the first day of school for twenty-three years in a row. Thank you for your unconditional love and support.

To Paige who consistently reminds me I have a gift and that my students are blessed. Thank you for helping me celebrate the good moments and for supporting me through the hard ones.

To Laur who always thinks of me more highly than I deserve. You've been my cheerleader from the start, singing my praises. Thank you for believing in me. (Now it's your turn. Publah shahbook.)

To my students who tell me I'm the bestest teacher in the whole wide world, even though you've only had two in your lifetime. You trust me, even when I don't know I'm doing. Thank you for inspiring me to be a better teacher and person.

To my God who has gifted me with natural abilities and drive. Thank you for equipping me to do what I do every day.

ABOUT THE AUTHOR

Tammy McMorrow has taught first grade for twenty-three years in Kuna, Idaho. She firmly believes she's ultimately in charge of her own professional development, and she's been blessed with the time, space, and energy to constantly learn and repeatedly outgrow her best teaching self throughout her career. She attributes much of her literacy pedagogy to Reading Recovery training during her third year of teaching. Working towards her master's in reading, as well as becoming a Boise State Writing Project fellow in 2006, extended her practice tremendously. Most recently she became an Idaho Coaching Network teacher. She'll be seeing the benefits of that professional experience for years to come.

Tammy has provided training at various levels and on various topics within her school and district. She has also presented regionally, as a Boise State Writing Project fellow and as an independent contractor.

When Tammy is not teaching or thinking about teaching, she's reading. She also loves to sing and has recorded three Christian CDs with her cousin, Laurie.

You can learn more about Tammy's classroom and practices by visiting her blog, Forever in First (foreverin1st@blogspot.com), or connecting with her on Twitter: @tammymcmorrow.

Made in the USA
Middletown, DE
28 June 2017